Cosmic Grooves:

Aquarius

by Jane Hodges

CHRONICLE BOOKS

SAN FRANCISCO

RHINO

Text copyright © 2001 Chronicle Books LLC
Executive Producer: Andrea Kinloch
Compilation Produced for Release: Dave Kapp, Mark Pinkus, and Andrea Kinloch
Remastering: Bob Fisher at Pacific Multimedia Corp.
Licensing: Wendi Cartwright
Project Assistance: Patrick Milligan, Amy Utstein, Mary Patton, and Mason Williams

Rhino Entertainment Company
10635 Santa Monica Blvd.
Los Angeles, California 90025
www.rhino.com

Library of Congress Cataloging-in-Publication Data available.
ISBN 0-8118-3054-3

Printed in China

Designed by Michael Mabry
Illustration © 2001 Michael Mabry

Distributed in Canada by Raincoast Books
9050 Shaughnessy Street
Vancouver, British Columbia V6P 6E5

10 9 8 7 6 5 4 3 2 1

Chronicle Books LLC
85 Second Street
San Francisco, California 94105
www.chroniclebooks.com

Aquarius
January 21 to February 20

Element: *Air*
Quality: *Fixed, a sign that provides consistency*
Motto: *"I theorize"*
Planetary Ruler: ♅ *Uranus, the planet of unexpected surprise and invention*
Uranus's Influence: *Inventive, expansive Uranus lends Aquarians a detached curiosity about people and communities. Always progressive, Aquarians enjoy advancing social change, scientific discovery, and humanitarian ideals. Eccentric at times, they often support unconventional causes and individuals. They have the power to transform an unlikely sounding inspiration into reality. Friendly, open-minded Aquarians make others feel at ease.*
Symbol: *Water Bearer*
Water Bearer's Influence: *Like the symbol of a man carrying water, the substance symbolizing human emotion, Aquarians keep themselves at arm's length from humanity's deepest emotions and urges. Their detached outlook gives them the ability to lead the masses while living among them, always maintaining just enough distance to create social progress and think effectively. While others may accuse them of avoiding intimacy, Aquarians rarely judge people unfairly and support group movements of all kinds.*

How to recognize an Aquarius:
Broad cheekbones, unconventional dress, eccentric opinions
Pick-up line: *"I feel like we've known each other in another life."*
What an Aquarius wants:
Community, philanthropy
What an Aquarius needs:
Identity, intimacy
Jukebox selection: *"You've Got a Friend"*

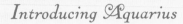

Introducing Aquarius

Aquarians are the zodiac's people lovers and social workers. Ruled by Uranus ♅, the planet of the unexpected, Aquarians like to stir controversy, especially the kind that will prompt social change. Their detached and friendly approach to communicating makes them effective reformers, and they often have many favorite social and political causes. Whether they attempt to shock or not, their goal is the same: Aquarians want to invent and promote innovative ways for people to live their lives. Born under an air sign, they are talkative, intellectual people who possess good communication and analysis skills and feel driven by a need to work within communities and improve them. Aquarians' warmth makes them effortlessly popular.

Children of this sign are outgoing, enjoy outings to public places, and thrive in groups. At times they will behave badly, but mostly because they enjoy testing the limits of those around them. As teens, Aquarians will experiment with rebellion in order to test reactions to their unconventional ideas. Young Aquarians are likely to wear their politics on their sleeve—often literally, by wearing clothes that make their parents blush. Even if they retain a mainstream appearance, they will most likely get involved in far-out causes or become activists at a young age. Other Aquarians apply their mental energies to their schoolwork, and they often emerge as good leaders and mediators.

In adulthood, Aquarians maintain friends from all walks of life, a trait that serves them well. They need to guard against overextending themselves financially and socially, though, as the typical Aquarian will offer the spare room, a generous loan, or a sympathetic ear without a second thought. In their spare time, Aquarians enjoy people-watching, exploring new neighborhoods, and foreign travel. As volunteers, they like mentoring children, working for charities, or counseling those in crisis. Political activities that put democracy to work also appeal to Aquarians, who can often be found circulating petitions or reminding people to vote. Many Aquarians are mechanically inclined and curious about technology, and they enjoy the idea of a "virtual" reality; where spending time at the computer is fun. To an Aquarius, life is a celebration of friendship and the power of community.

Dedicated to Aquarius

Aquarians love new ideas and diverse groups of people. They'll like tunes that pose rhetorical questions or experiment with new forms of sound.

Liberal	Water Bearers are devoted fans of individual freedom and universal acceptance, and *Aquarius* by The 5th Dimension celebrates their lofty ideals.
Popular	*I'll Be Around* sung by the Spinners acknowledges this sign's social availability to others. Aquarians are never ones to turn down an invitation.
Dependable	Water Bearers never shun the chance to help a friend in need, and *Bridge over Troubled Water* sung by Aretha Franklin is an ode to the support this sign offers others.
Loyal	Aquarians are quick to forgive faults and constantly delight in their friends. *You've Got a Friend* sung by Donny Hathaway is an ode to this sign's deep commitment to friendships of all kinds.
Entertaining	*Get Together* performed by The Youngbloods is the perfect Aquarian party song since Water Bearers love to see people from different backgrounds making connections.
Kind	Aquarians treat all their friends with equal respect, and would not hesitate to help a stranger. *He Ain't Heavy,*

He's My Brother sung by Glen Campbell is an ode to Water Bearers' open-minded approach.

Globally conscious
Worldly Aquarians see commonalities—rather than differences—among different cultures. *New World* by Karla Bonoff applauds their universal understanding of mankind.

Radical
Often outspoken advocates or activists, Water Bearers will defend a cause they believe in. *Rebels Are We* by Chic celebrates Aquarian bravery and social change.

Technical
Cerebral Aquarians embrace technology and *She Blinded Me with Science* by Thomas Dolby celebrates their enthusiasm for innovation.

Unconventional
This sign delights in the unexpected and adores experimentation, and *Weird Science* by Oingo Boingo describes the Aquarian love of quirkiness.

Humanitarian
Aquarians feel everyone should enjoy basic freedoms, and will give of their time to advance society. *Volunteers* by Jefferson Airplane toasts their philanthropy.

Utopian
From free and unstructured to accepting and argumentative, the archetypes of the Aquarius persona are celebrated in *Aquarius* by Cannonball Adderley.

Aquarius at Work

While their eccentric nature suggests that they're not well suited to the conventional corporate world, Aquarian people skills give these folks a knack for managing and facilitating teams at work. These individuals prefer coming up with big-picture ideas to managing day-to-day issues. Because invention and discovery are important to this sign, working in research and development appeals to Aquarians—especially if the position is a fellowship or paid sabbatical, since they prefer to have as much independence as possible. Water Bearers may espouse some very unusual ways of getting their work done, but if they find a higher-up to support their ideas and handle the commercial side of things they can succeed. Their cultural savvy gives them an accurate sense of how people feel about any given issue, and they enjoy working with the public directly or indirectly. They are driven more by values than money, and while at times their way of doing things clashes with convention, they have the tenacity to prove their detractors wrong and persevere to the finish line.

Those born under this idea-driven sign enjoy serving the public and influencing public opinion. Aquarian Arthur Ochs Sulzberger publishes the widely read *New York Times*, while Water Bearer Charles Schwab formed a world-renowned brokerage that made investing easily accessible to the public. Because they enjoy observing and analyzing people's behavior, Aquarians succeed as anthropologists, group coordinators, human resources professionals, executive recruiters, or market researchers. However, because they need to believe their work helps others, humanitarian positions appeal more. They flock to programs like the Peace Corps. Aquarians make excellent nonprofit administrators, union organizers, and professional fund raisers. In general, any career involving public outreach is up their alley. Aquarians also excel in the sciences and technology. In fact, Sir Francis Bacon, the inventor of the scientific method, was an Aquarius. Jobs in aeronautics, aviation, or other types of mechanical engineering appeal to those under this sign, as do roles at new media and Internet companies where teamwork is essential.

Aquarius in Love

Independent-minded Aquarians want a mate who doubles as a best friend and is capable of maintaining separate interests. That doesn't mean Aquarians merely want a platonic relationship with benefits. They need to understand their partner as a friend before they can fall in love, and even once they're in a serious relationship, they like to maintain a certain levity and freshness that characterized the union's earlier stages. An Aquarian's attraction to a partner is based on a mental connection—shared values regarding independence, freedom, and the rights of individuals to live as they wish—as well as a physical attraction. The ultimate expression of partnership for an Aquarian is to be able to share group activities with a mate. While Water Bearers dispense with conventional romantic gestures, they shower a mate with inventive and oddly endearing surprises. They don't do well with possessive or secretive partners who demand constant one-on-one attention. Rarely demanding themselves, Aquarians need a partner who will remind them of their commitment to romance while also allowing them philosophical and emotional freedom.

Aquarius Relationships

Aquarius & Aries (*March 21 to April 20*)   Passionate

Aquarius & Taurus (*April 21 to May 21*)   Challenging

Aquarius & Gemini (*May 22 to June 21*)   Passionate

Aquarius & Cancer (*June 22 to July 22*)   Harmonious

Aquarius & Leo (*July 23 to August 23*)   Passionate

Aquarius & Virgo (*August 24 to September 22*)   Challenging

Aquarius & Libra (*September 23 to October 23*)   Passionate

Aquarius & Scorpio (*October 24 to November 22*)   Challenging

Aquarius & Sagittarius (*November 23 to December 21*)   Passionate

Aquarius & Capricorn (*December 22 to January 20*)   Harmonious

Aquarius & Aquarius (*January 21 to February 20*)   Harmonious

Aquarius & Pisces (*February 21 to March 20*)   Challenging

She can be friendly and approachable, like Aquarians
Jennifer Aniston and Geena Davis, or offbeat
and mysterious, like Water Bearers Christina Ricci and
Heather Graham. Independent and imaginative, this cerebral
lady wants a man who stirs her mind as well as her emotions.
He'll have to respect her intellectually, and possess a
mind that she can respect, in order for the relationship to last.
The right man for her will be attentive, humanitarian, and
kind, yet independent enough to allow her the
freedom her intellectual and social pursuits require.

Aquarius Woman & Aries Man

Natalie Cole seeks Luther Vandross.

Things click from the start. Chatty Miss Aquarius and the sociable Ram are both optimists. She loves his passionate commitment to his interests, but can temper it with her rational approach. Proud Mr. Aries will share his deepest secrets with her, since she's nonjudgmental and open-minded. At times, she'll have to remind him not to be so self-centered, and that he'll make more of an impact when he shares the stage. He'll remind her of her priorities, including spending time alone with him, even though he admires the way she effortlessly maintains a wide circle of friends. Mr. Aries loves her sociable side and enjoys the challenge of pursuing this much sought-after siren. In turn, Miss Aquarius appreciates his directness and the way he makes a beeline for his goals—especially when his goal is coaxing commitment out of her. Sexually, he's as daring as she is open-minded, and they can take each other to new and exciting places in the bedroom. This pair can go anywhere and feel right at home—in fact, they may decide soon after the first date that the best place to live is together.

Aquarius Woman & Taurus Man

Sheryl Crow seeks Billy Squier.

Straightforward Mr. Taurus can spend his life in one room, while airy Miss Aquarius needs lots of room to roam. Still, she respects his stability and the way he's faithful to friends and commitments. Conversely, he likes the way she gets him out of his routines and into new things like language classes or exotic cooking. The problem from her point of view is that he tilts towards routine, while she's an idea person whose flights of fancy lead to literal flights from one activity to the next. Yet, since friendship is the basis for Aquarian love relationships, this duo's mutual respect gives them lasting love potential. If Mr. Taurus opens his mind and realizes that security is a global rather than an individual concern, and Miss Aquarius settles down and realizes that changing the world requires a secure home base, these two are in for smooth sailing. Their friendly rapport, which works as well in the bedroom as it does elsewhere, will keep them together for years to come. Even if their home is filled with half-finished projects, their love for one another is one thing they're committed to building—and it is likely to last a lifetime.

Aquarius Woman & Gemini Man

Etta James seeks Benny Goodman.

If they meet at a Halloween party, each wearing a fantastic costume culled from an ancient fairy tale, Miss Aquarius and Mr. Gemini will be the only people in the room who recognize each other's character. These two extroverts love people and make a fantastic match. Their rapport works as well on an intimate level as it does when they're surrounded by their diverse flock of friends. They'll accompany one another everywhere, promote the same obscure charities, shop at the local co-op, and volunteer at the local soup kitchen. Miss Aquarius and Mr. Gemini love to talk and will discuss everything, especially their favorite liberal causes. This dynamic duo makes good company and will be highly popular. If they can get a moment alone, they will remember they make excellent lovers—they never cease to surprise one another. Their only argument will be over how big a wedding to have. Should they rent out Central Park, or the entire island of Manhattan?

Aquarius Woman & Cancer Man

Carole King seeks Marc Cohn.

She likes a man who isn't afraid to express his feelings, and in Mr. Cancer she finds the original sensitive New Age man. He supports her altruism and need to participate in social causes. However, for this relationship to work, she'll have to teach him to look beyond domesticity for happiness. Miss Aquarius considers the world her family and sees no need to marry and settle down, while Mr. Cancer can't imagine devoting himself to public life without first securing a loving mate. If he can convince her that she's a better humanitarian when she has a steady, intimate home life, they can find a compromise that satisfies both of them. Her allowing him to handle the finances, which she might squander carelessly, and voicing appreciation for his stability make this intuitive man feel needed. These two won't have to work hard to enjoy a friendly relationship that could lead to life-long commitment. Sexually, he's sensitive and creative, and over time he'll adjust to her more experimental style. This empathetic couple will live in tune with the times and each other.

Aquarius Woman & Leo Man

Eartha Kitt seeks Tony Bennett.

♂ ♀

This fun, funny couple will see sparks the moment they meet. She is touched by the pride he takes in making his own unique and indelible mark on the world. His approach is the opposite of sociable and selfless Miss Aquarius, who defines herself through her relationships to others. Because of this, sexy Mr. Leo can teach her to value her individuality—the way she looks, thinks, and acts—in a new light. He flatters her, makes her laugh, and helps her realize she's as important as her constellation of friends and loved ones. Conversely, she teaches him to look at the world as a gathering place big enough for many egos, not just his own, and that sometimes giving others the stage is more valuable than grandstanding. She'll be surprised at his jealousy; her flirty friendliness is a challenge he must overcome. The physical fireworks that result from their union will deeply satisfy both of them. Since they're both optimists, they can work out any differences—and are destined to share a long life of parties and passion.

Aquarius Woman & Virgo Man

Jody Watley seeks Van Morrison.

The zodiac's most polite man and this friendly far-out woman share a humanitarian spirit. Miss Aquarius may not agree with Mr. Virgo's systematic way of doing things, but she knows instinctively that his heart's in the right place and he has only good intentions. This shy Mercury-ruled guy finds her easy to talk to, if a bit eccentric, and he likes the way she's open-minded enough to listen to his ideas. He wants to organize the world, while she wants to introduce revolutionary change. Naturally, his conservatism and her anarchical tendencies make each other nervous, but if they decide to overlook political differences they'll find they have a lot in common. Sexually, his earthy and gentle approach inspires her sensual side, while her offbeat attitude sparks his experimental streak. If they can agree on financial matters, a long-term commitment could work well, since he'll grant her the freedom she needs and she'll hand him the organizational reins in the relationship. In this democratic partnership, both sides will win at love.

Aquarius Woman & Libra Man

Yoko Ono seeks John Lennon.

When her gift for shock value meets his gift for diplomacy, these two could introduce some radical ideas to the world—and see them become part of popular culture. They could also just discuss the possibilities. These two share a love of social causes and can talk for hours. While Miss Aquarius will join the Million Woman March, Mr. Libra tends to favor compromise and tries to please the majority. Still, she loves the idea of this smart, diplomatic man using his intelligence to create social change. Sexually, his willingness to please and her inventive ideas lead to hours of rapture. They both feel relieved that they've found a friend, business partner, and companion who understands the need for freedom. While marriage isn't a very revolutionary institution as far as Miss Aquarius is concerned, she's willing to join open-minded Mr. Libra in a unique union where good ideas and friendship take center stage.

Aquarius Woman & Scorpio Man

Marian Anderson seeks Johnny Mercer.

He's dark, secretive, and keeps a low profile. She's sweet, guileless, and talks to everybody. Inner-directed Mr. Scorpio tries to transform himself and the world, while outer-directed Miss Aquarius thrives in social environments where she can transform a group. In this case, opposites attract. She likes his near-compulsive focus on his personal and professional goals, and he's drawn to her levity and sociability. As a couple, he can help her focus away from the many distractions and characters who take up her time, while she can soften his occasionally bitter edge and teach him to share her goofy sense of humor. While Miss Aquarius has a wide and ever-growing circle of acquaintances, Mr. Scorpio can help her separate the dependable, deep relationships from the superficial and merely entertaining ones. Sexually, he's expressive and passionate while she's experimental and free. Together, they can spend a lifetime trying to understand each other—and laughing at the unexpected good results.

Aquarius Woman & Sagittarius Man

Juice Newton seeks Randy Newman.

There's no question that this is a winning duo. Sociable Miss Aquarius and the fun-loving, philosophical Archer man make an excellent match. The lady Water Bearer appreciates that Mr. Sagittarius never gets jealous or questions her eccentricities and shares her need for freedom. He won't mind if she's running a commune in the attic and a petting zoo in the backyard, nor will she flinch when he tells her sordid and fantastical tales of his travels. In bed, he's suggestive and adventurous, and she's open-minded enough to try anything he suggests. He's direct enough to pull her away from her perpetual crowd of friends when he senses she needs a break, and his idea of a good time jibes well with hers. Both love travel and adventure, and learning about other cultures. They'll be the life of any party they attend—and they'll attend every party they're invited to. There's never a dull moment for this unstoppable pair.

Aquarius Woman & Capricorn Man

Melissa Manchester seeks Rod Stewart.

These two are so comfortable with each other that they may overlook the love potential beneath their easygoing friendship. Miss Aquarius finds him a bit earnest and buttoned-up for her tastes, but he's uncomplicated and she trusts him. Mr. Capricorn's serious outlook and dry humor make her laugh, and she likes to try to get him to lighten up. He respects her social awareness, her intelligence, and the way she treats friends like family. While his pragmatism can clash with her idealism, rather than fight over their differences these two may become fond of their dissimilarities. They innately know how to give each other space to cultivate outside interests, so the time they spend together feels special. His down-to-earth approach to relationships relaxes the analytical Water Bearer—especially in bed. Over time, she will appreciate his earnestness, especially as he grows more socially accepting under her influence. His conventional success and her unconventional perspectives will make them a sought-after couple. This pair will find as much harmony at home as with friends.

Aquarius Woman & Aquarius Man

Chynna Phillips seeks Steve Perry.

Few folks can better befriend an Aquarius than another Aquarius. They tend to show up in the same unconventional places and have the same eccentric friends, and when they meet they'll appreciate each other instantly. These two will quickly cut through subtle diplomacy and honestly reveal their unusual opinions to one another. In bed, they really know how to please one another, and both are willing to act out their fantasies. If they move in together, they'll allow one another the freedom each needs—after all, when both mates have a constant stream of guests passing through, life feels a bit like an open-ended forum of creative new ideas. These two are impractical and idealistic, and will travel far and wide to learn and expand their knowledge. They'll have to find a way to ground each other, as both of them enjoy new directions and philosophical experiments. In the end, though, the constant in this relationship is the one that matters: they will love and respect each other as friends and life mates.

Aquarius Woman & Pisces Man

Roberta Flack seeks Nat King Cole.

Romantic Mr. Pisces and quirky Miss Aquarius are both dreamers, though different kinds. He takes an escapist, artistic approach to life, sometimes preferring his imagination to reality. It will take an outside force to kick-start their relationship, because both of them have a way of idling while friends drive past them on the highway of life. If they sense attraction, though, and make an effort to understand one another, things can work out well for these two. She likes her freedom, and his changeable nature means he vacillates between social groups. He's attracted to her warmth and intelligence and will share her passion for humanitarian causes. She's attracted to his sensitivity and depth, though at times she'll have a hard time understanding his need to withdraw from life's rich pageant she so enjoys. In bed, he's suggestive and mysterious, while she is talkative and wacky. They're both creative, though, so over time they'll learn how to please each other. Neither of them is practical, but that's why this pair is so wonderful. If they make their relationship a priority, they'll learn that love can revolutionize both their lives.

Mr. Aquarius and His Women

He can be appealing and friendly, like Aquarians
Paul Newman and Tom Selleck, or outrageous
and provocative, like Water Bearers Chris Rock and
Arsenio Hall. In either case, he needs a liberal
woman with a mind he can respect. The right woman
for him will lead an enriching life of her own
and know not to demand a commitment too early
in the game. If she can allow him his
freedom and forgive his mistakes, he will delight
her with his creative approach to romance.
He wants a lover who doubles as a life-long friend.

Aquarius Man & Aries Woman

Garth Brooks seeks Emmylou Harris.

Mr. Aquarius likes people who are positive, adventurous, and have a zest for life, and go-getter Miss Aries fits the bill. Separating this man from his crowd presents a major task, but she will enjoy the challenge. He'll be flattered when she makes her move and pleasantly surprised by how much fun they have alone, as well as together in one of his many groups of friends. She applauds the way he follows his unconventional ideals, and he can teach her to think more expansively and use her sparkling personality to serve causes rather than herself. Mr. Aquarius will find the Ram woman endlessly intriguing, while she'll always remain engaged by the challenge of capturing his undivided attention. Physically, this daring woman will teach him erotic tricks even this experimental guy has never imagined. They both dislike authority and tradition, so they'll share a rebellious sense of humor. This lively duo will reveal their love to one another in surprising ways that keep their romance fresh. The continuing novelty of being together will keep them dancing through the years.

Aquarius Man & Taurus Woman

Sonny Bono seeks Cher.

He lives for intellectual stimulation and political causes; she lives for physical comforts and material security. At first, they see one another through rose-colored glasses. Mr. Aquarius perceives this quiet woman as an open-minded liberal who will accompany him as he rallies troops and participates in the latest social movements or political fads. Miss Taurus assumes this charismatic, popular man will make a good provider who could share a life with her and also make her laugh. One day, however, they may recognize the reality: He has no intention of orienting his life around a quest for mere material security, while she has no intention of chucking it all to march for world peace. If they keep a sense of humor, though, they can reach a surprisingly pleasant compromise. He can teach her that he wants to give her a better ideological world to live in, and she can give him a solid home in the world he wants to improve. They'll have a lifetime of surprises learning to understand one another.

Aquarius Man & Gemini Woman

Axl Rose seeks Stevie Nicks.

These two recognize in one another a love of people. That Mr. Aquarius is perpetually surrounded by others is all the more appealing to charismatic Miss Gemini, who naturally understands his affection for the crowd. They'll talk late into the night unless they're enjoying their zesty physical compatibility or tending to a friend in crisis. Together, they'll be a mercurial pair. The process of thinking through the possibilities may, for these two, provide more fun than the solutions themselves. Their dynamic may appear a bit wild and immature to some people, but this couple likes the freedom they give each other. Variety is the spice of life for these two—especially in the bedroom, where their creativity shines. A strong friendship will serve as the foundation for their love. Both prize a companion who is easygoing and flexible, as well as intellectual and exciting, and in each other they will find it. This exuberant pair loves being together. In each other, they've found a beloved partner who sets them free.

Aquarius Man & Cancer Woman

Kurt Cobain seeks Courtney Love.

He finds this emotional, loving woman endearing. Both are intensely loyal to friends and like to be there for other people. The problem here is that Miss Cancer plays a bit closer to the vest, both socially and financially, than Mr. Aquarius. She rarely lets newcomers into her inner sanctum—or her home—without getting to know them, while he'll open his doors and wallet to strangers. She's conservative with cash, while he reasons that you can't take it with you and spends freely. If he lets her keep a separate bank account so she can monitor their rainy-day backup, she can get beyond this hurdle in their relationship. Since he has an urge to protect vulnerable Miss Cancer rather than to pal around with her in his typical chummy fashion, their sex life may lack the openness and daring he's used to with more easygoing partners. With work, though, this pair can find satisfaction. If they discover how to keep the relationship lively for him and secure for her, their shared empathy and intuition toward each other will make them a wise and happy couple.

Aquarius Man & Leo Woman

Peter Gabriel seeks Tori Amos.

Mr. Aquarius and Miss Leo are opposites who attract. He'll find the lady Lioness sexy, vibrant, and creative, yet he'll see her need to distinguish herself all the time as a narcissistic exercise. She'll consider his earnest social and political conscience a character flaw and encourage him to take to the limelight. If these two meet and connect, though, she can actually teach selfless Mr. Aquarius that he has a vibrant personality worth expressing for its own sake, rather than always being directed to the good of some group or cause. In turn, he can teach sassy Miss Leo that she could better connect to her audience if she listened to them more and performed for them less. In bed, her focus and his experimentation make for hours of pleasure. These two challenge each other, but in a healthy way. Their differences soften over time as their love for one another grows.

Aquarius Man & Virgo Woman

Phil Collins seeks Patsy Cline.

♀ ♂

These two share a cerebral but friendly rapport. Rebellious Mr. Aquarius finds it touching that she likes helping people become more efficient when his approach is to encourage others to rebel against social conventions. Her proper friends and good manners, paired with his wild friends and eccentric opinions, make an odd combination to say the least. At times, they don't make sense to each other. Mr. Aquarius loves the chaos that leads to revolutionary change, while Miss Virgo loves the order that assures propriety. Yet they do appreciate and respect their shared interest in helping other people. This relationship will work better if she remains open-minded, for he can be dissenting and contrary. Nonetheless, he's flexible enough to accept her criticism objectively and work to share a life that's secure socially and financially in order to keep her. His tolerance is a relief to Miss Virgo, who is as critical of herself as she is of those around her. Mr. Aquarius will inspire her to take risks, and staying in a long-lasting relationship with him is one that will almost surely pay off.

35

Aquarius Man & Libra Woman

Neil Diamond seeks Toni Braxton.

The most rebellious man in the zodiac and agreeable Miss Libra make a surprisingly good couple. They'll experience almost instant physical attraction and, while commitment-shy Mr. Aquarius may initially resist falling for this diplomatic siren, he'll soon discover that beneath her polite persona she is a true catch. In fact, she's perfect for him. She's sociable, tolerant, open-minded, and interested in celebrating intelligent ideas—especially in bed, where they feel at ease experimenting. She'll support his changing devotion to social causes and his shifting professional interests since she prizes expansive, flexible thinking. He likes to talk about things as much as she does, and their rapport will be open and enviable. While Mr. Aquarius tends to avoid rushing into a relationship, the fact that Miss Libra allows him his coveted freedom will make him as eager to tie the knot as she is. There will be few conflicts, save her reaction to his occasional social eccentricities, and lots of good times for these two.

Aquarius Man & Scorpio Woman

Wofgang Mozart seeks Mahalia Jackson.

These two zodiacal opposites attract—and arouse each other's curiosity. She's drawn to people's private passions, while he's intrigued by their public personae. Her idea of intimacy is making love for an entire weekend in a secluded lakeside cabin; his idea of closeness is having his partner nearby while he talks to everyone else—he likes to have his "freedom" and his relationship in motion simultaneously. It would be accurate to assume that these two have their work cut out for them. She's more security-minded than he is, and she doesn't understand his constant need to be part of the swirling masses. Yet she appreciates his open-minded attitude. After all, Miss Scorpio has an enigmatic quality that many men fear—but not Mr. Aquarius. He's so open-minded, in fact, he'll decide to give Scorpio-style love a try. She's passionate in bed, seductive on a dance floor, and intellectually mesmerizing. It won't be easy for either of them, but neither will it be dull. If they decide to give this relationship their best efforts, they might end up finding long-lasting fire.

Aquarius Man & Sagittarius Woman

Rick James seeks Tina Turner.

It will take a long time for these two to meet since they're both constantly surrounded by friends, but the minute they start talking they'll feel like they've met a fellow old soul. Miss Sagittarius is good-looking, friendly, adventurous, and could care less about traditional definitions of security. If Mr. Aquarius can stop talking with her long enough to kiss her, she'll be delighted. Together they're the life of any party and the galvanizers behind every cause. Where he lacks focus, she has the drive to put him firmly back on course. Where she lacks tact, he smooths over the situation with his sociability. This unconventional pair makes up their own rules as they go along. In bed, energetic Miss Sagittarius and erotic Mr. Aquarius know how to have a great time. They're the most outgoing couple in town, and will have the wildest wedding party anyone's ever attended.

Aquarius Man & Capricorn Woman

Seal seeks Sade.

Miss Capricorn and this unpredictable air sign share a friendly energy that often remains just that—friendship, but sometimes this friendship can form a strong basis for love. If they do fall for one another, it will take a long time. Mr. Aquarius fears diving into something too intimate too quickly, because he needs room in his life for his many social causes and friends. She won't commit until she's sure she can trust him, and she won't trust this unpredictable man unless she's known him for years. She likes his social awareness and his open-minded approach. Since she judges herself harshly, she appreciates his enthusiasm and support. She won't, however, like the way he experiments with his vocation and sometimes fails to bring home a regular paycheck. He's turned on by her undeniable smarts. Since Miss Capricorn holds her own financially, intellectually, and socially, Mr. Aquarius feels free to do his own thing, which is just what he needs. This relationship of equals satisfies both of them with its balance of independence and passion.

Aquarius Man & Aquarius Woman

Alice Cooper seeks Baby Spice.

They've made the same obscure pilgrimages, have seen the same cult movies, and have the same radical bumper stickers pasted on their cars. These two ego-free eccentrics genuinely appreciate each other, though their similarities may not provide the friction a love relationship needs to ignite. However, since friendship often begets love for Aquarians, they may fall in love over time. Because Mr. and Miss Aquarius are both devoted to changing society, they can accept in each other all the unconventional behavior that past partners have feared. Sexually, they are experimental and straightforward, with few emotional or physical hangups between them. On a day-to-day basis they will be surrounded socially—and there's a danger that their friends will know more about this union than the Aquarian partners themselves. However, since community is so important to these two, their open-door policy towards friends will likely bolster the romance rather than derail it. If they decide to commit, they can look forward to changing each other's worlds, as well as the world around them.

Aquarius Man & Pisces Woman

Warren Zevon seeks Nina Hagen.

The quirky Aquarian man and romantic Miss Pisces can make a good match, but they'll have to work for it. This is a highly impractical pair, as both are focused on saving the world in different ways. She has a great deal of empathy and an elusive, potent imagination, but at times, her emotional response clashes with his detached one. He maintains that detachment because it helps him accomplish his lofty ideological goals for world change. The result is that when she needs a pat on the back, he may be off rallying the troops for social justice. She'll listen when he needs to talk about his next great idea, but will always be surprised by his ability to stay at arm's length from his feelings. In bed, they're both experimental and generous, and over time, they can grow close. On a day-to-day basis though, they'll have their work cut out for them. Giving time to their relationship, however, may be the best cause either could commit to. With some effort, they can become passionately important to one another.

Aquarius at Home

The Aquarius home is large and informal and filled with quirky furniture, high-tech gadgets, and gifts from the many friends those born under this sign typically keep. Like those born under other air signs, Aquarians need a lot of space to entertain and host guests, and they tend to share it with astounding generosity. Pull-out sofas and extra guest rooms are necessary to house the constant stream of visitors. The Aquarian decorating style tends toward the eclectic. Electronic paraphernalia fits naturally with the crackling energy of their dwellings, and Aquarians love the latest handheld organizers, laptops, and cell phones, as well as more retro pop culture items like neon signs and old jukeboxes. They'll decorate in vibrant colors—perhaps this sign's trademark bright blue—that stimulate cheerful thoughts and conversation. They'll need a spare room for their eccentric hobbies. Aquarians enjoy both city and country living as long as they feel central—they like being close to social and cultural epicenters. They see no need for life in a gated community or elite neighborhood. The Aquarian home is where all are welcome to party, rest, or discuss progressive ideas.

Aquarius Health

Aquarius rules the lower legs and ankles as well as the circulatory system, which means this sign is vulnerable to leg and ankle injuries as well as colds. When Water Bearers get sick, their illnesses often come on suddenly, but they also tend to heal rapidly. Most Aquarians find great strength and joy in their friendships and group social activities. More introverted or rebellious Water Bearers can be depression-prone, as prolonged periods of isolation or misunderstanding stifle their naturally communicative nature. Especially as parents of young children, Aquarians are prone to their community's local viruses and infections, as they will always host the elementary school picnics and sleepovers. Because Aquarians need to keep their circulation going, walking is a good form of exercise for them, especially right after a meal. Alternatively, they might want to eat lightly and often, rather than consume three substantial meals each day. This sign is not always as physically coordinated as others, so exercise that is basic and repetitive can be effective for Aquarians, especially when they work out as part of a social group that cycles or hikes.

Aquarius Style

The Aquarius look tends to be casual and democratic. Both male and female Aquarians dress to fit in with people of all walks of life. While they may not have a distinct style, they may use their own body as a billboard for social causes, eschewing fur or snakeskin that involves cruelty to animals or boycotting commercial brands that use third-world sweatshops. Political T-shirts or pendants are seen by this sign as accessories. Younger Aquarians often wear clothes that shock in an attempt to make a social statement, and even more mature Aquarians may dress eccentrically, wearing funky clothes they found at thrift stores or cool items they made themselves. These people have too much on their minds to fuss in front of a mirror every morning, so they dress for a day that holds unexpected twists and turns. In general, Aquarians prefer casual outfits to formal or professional ones and rarely dress up just for fun. Their special color is a bright, electric blue that symbolizes intense thinking and brotherly love. Their special stone is the amethyst.

On the Road with Aquarius

Aquarians don't like the idea of voyeuristic tourism or lazy, insulated days at a luxury resort. Their idea of travel is more anthropological: They want to meet and mingle with foreign cultures and absorb different cultural mores and values, without intruding on them. Aquarians love foreign travel, especially to desert climates in Africa or South America, and they will try to document their journey by taking photos or keeping a diary. They also love annual festivals for film and art, so trips to Sundance or Cannes would appeal to them. Those born under this sign love volunteer work and may choose to vacation at an archaeological dig's site or an Israeli kibbutz. Environments where people with different backgrounds come together to work on a common goal are their idea of a good time. The ideal Aquarian vacation, even for grown Water Bearers, replicates the camp or field trip experience, where sharing and learning about a culture's day-to-day reality takes precedence over traditional tourist activities like shopping or visiting museums.

Aquarian social events are casual and spontaneous, yet even at the last minute, Aquarians can pull off a large party because they know so many people and can rally the troops easily. Water Bearers want their guests to mingle, and they like to host potlucks where everyone gets to be the chef. An outdoor picnic or rooftop wine party appeals to the Aquarian sense of fun. For this sign, friends are as important as family. Aquarian parties are a delight, because they will include people from all walks of life. Guests can expect to meet someone totally out of the ordinary when they attend an Aquarian fiesta. These parties also tend to get wild. Aquarians love it when friends tango on the coffee table, drink wine out of jelly jars, or sneak off to the far corners of the yard to share a cigar or a smooch. The name of the game is unpredictability, which is why Aquarian social events are so much fun.

In the Company of Aquarius

Musicians:
Anita Baker
Sonny Bono
Garth Brooks
Kurt Cobain
Natalie Cole
Alice Cooper
Sheryl Crow
Neil Diamond
Placido Domingo
Dr. Dre
Jacqueline Du Pré
Fabian
Roberta Flack
Peter Gabriel
Michael Hutchence (INXS)
Ice-T
Rick James
Carole King
Eartha Kitt
Bob Marley
Wolfgang Mozart
Juice Newton
Billy Ocean
Yoko Ono
Chynna Phillips
Johnny Rotten (Sex Pistols)
Franz Schubert
Eddie Van Halen
Jody Watley
Lucinda Williams

Performers:
Alan Alda
Jennifer Aniston
John Belushi
Linda Blair
Humphrey Bogart
Cindy Crawford
Ellen DeGeneres
Laura Dern
Mia Farrow
Farrah Fawcett
Clark Gable
Gene Hackman
Florence Henderson
Piper Laurie
Jack Lemmon
Paul Newman
Nick Nolte
Kim Novak
Vanessa Redgrave
Burt Reynolds
Christina Ricci
Chris Rock
Rene Russo
Telly Savalas
Tom Selleck
Cybil Shepherd
Lili Taylor
John Travolta
Oprah Winfrey

Reformers:
Sir Francis Bacon
Charles Darwin
Thomas Edison
Germaine Greer
Jimmy Hoffa
Abraham Lincoln
Charles Lindbergh
Douglas MacArthur
Sir Thomas More
Rosa Parks
Ronald Reagan
Franklin D. Roosevelt

Artists:
Ansel Adams
Robert Altman
Jules Feiffer
Matt Groening
Edouard Manet
Robert Motherwell
Jackson Pollock
Norman Rockwell

Athletes:
Hank Aaron
Mikhail Baryshnikov
Wayne Gretzky
Michael Jordan
Greg Louganis
John McEnroe
Jack Nicklaus
Mary Lou Retton
Jackie Robinson
Babe Ruth
Fran Tarkenton

Writers:
Jean Auel
Paul Auster
Judy Blume
Bertolt Brecht
William S. Burroughs
Lewis Carroll
Colette
Charles Dickens
James Dickey
Richard Ford
John Grisham
Langston Hughes
James Joyce
Sinclair Lewis
Norman Mailer
William Somerset Maugham
James A. Michener
Toni Morrison
Chaim Potok
Ayn Rand
Ruth Rendell
Sidney Sheldon
Gertrude Stein
Alice Walker
Edith Wharton
Virginia Woolf

Permissions

Aquarius/Let the Sunshine In
The 5th Dimension
(Galt MacDermot/James Rado/Gerome Ragni)
Courtesy of BMG Special Products.

I'll Be Around
Spinners
(Thom Bell/Phil Hurtt)
℗ 1972 Atlantic Recording Corp., produced under license
from Atlantic Recording Corp.

Bridge over Troubled Water
Aretha Franklin
(Paul Simon)
Produced under license from Atlantic Recording Corp.

You've Got a Friend
Donny Hathaway
(Carole King)
Produced under license from Elektra Entertainment Group.

Get Together
The Youngbloods
(Chet Powers)
Courtesy of BMG Special Products.

He Ain't Heavy, He's My Brother
Glen Campbell
(Bobby Scott/Bob Russell)
Under license from EMI-Capitol Music Special Markets.

New World
Karla Bonoff
(Karla Bonoff)
℗ 1988 Gold Castle Records, courtesy of Karla Bonoff.

Rebels Are We
Chic
(Bernard Edwards/Nile Rodgers)
℗ 1980 Atlantic Recording Corp., produced under license from
Atlantic Recording Corp.

She Blinded Me with Science
Thomas Dolby
(Thomas Dolby/Joe Kerr)
℗ 1982 Capitol Records, Inc., under license from
EMI-Capitol Music Special Markets.

Weird Science
Oingo Boingo
(Danny Elfman)
℗ 1985 MCA Records, Inc., courtesy of Universal Music
Special Markets, Inc.

Volunteers
Jefferson Airplane
(Marty Balin/Paul Kantner)
Courtesy of BMG Special Products.

Aquarius
Cannonball Adderley featuring The Nat Adderley Sextet
(Mike Deasy/Rick Holmes)
℗ 1972 Capitol Records, Inc., under license from EMI-Capitol
Music Special Markets.

This Compilation ℗ 2001 Rhino Entertainment Company.

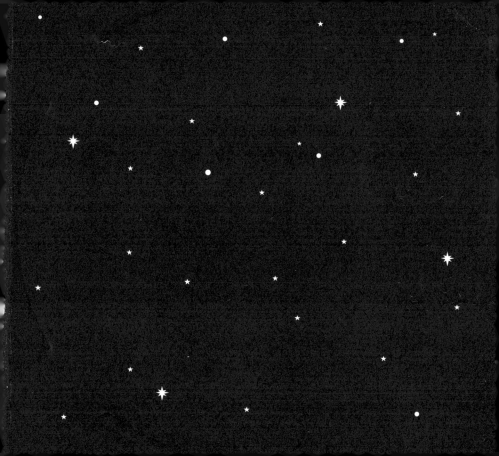

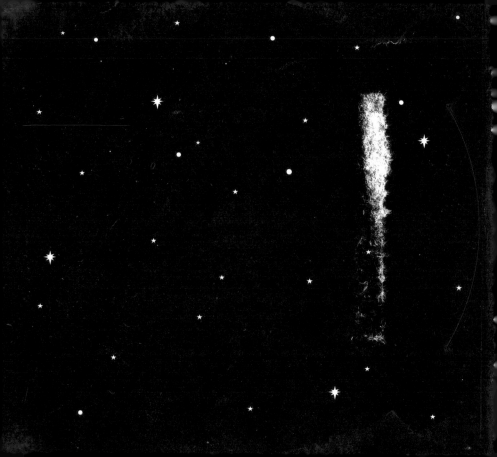

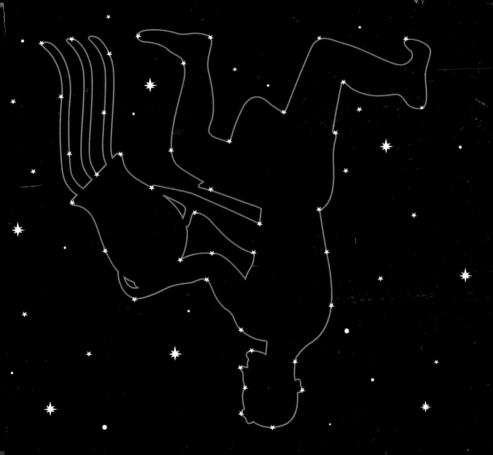

Aquarius

Cosmic Grooves: